Let's Learn to Pray

Talk to God about Anything and Everything

ZONDERkidz

ZONDERKIDZ

The Beginner's Bible® Let's Learn to Pray
Copyright © 2023 by Zonderkidz
Illustrations © 2023, 2022, 2016 by Zonderkidz

Requests for information should be addressed to:
Zonderkidz, 3900 *Sparks Drive SE, Grand Rapids, Michigan* 49546

ISBN 978-0-310-14191-4 (hardcover)
ISBN 978-0-310-14192-1 (ebook)

Library of Congress Cataloging-in-Publication Data

Names: Zonderkidz
Title: The beginner's Bible let's learn to pray : talk to God about anything and everything.
Other titles: Let's learn to pray
Description: Grand Rapids, Michigan : Zonderkidz, 2023. | Audience: Ages
    4-8 | Summary: "Start children on the path to a fulfilling, lifelong
    prayer habit. The Beginner's Bible is a perennial favorite with young
    children and their parents, impacting 25 million families for over 30
    years. Now The Beginner's Bible Let's Learn to Pray offers young
    children an interactive introduction to prayer, showing them that they
    can talk to God about anything and everything. Featuring helpful
    examples from classic Bible stories, children will learn the basics of
    prayer, including why we pray and how to pray. With fun prompts,
    accessible questions, and bright, colorful illustrations, kids will be
    eager to talk to God about their daily experiences, and will learn how
    to listen to His still, small voice"– Provided by publisher.
Identifiers: LCCN 2022013429 (print) | LCCN 2022013430 (ebook) |
    ISBN 9780310141914 (hardcover) | ISBN 9780310141921 (ebook)
Subjects: LCSH: Prayer–Christianity–Juvenile literature.
Classification: LCC BV212 .B44 2023 (print) | LCC BV212 (ebook) |
    DDC 248.3/2–dc23/eng/20220801
LC record available at https://lccn.loc.gov/2022013429
LC ebook record available at https://lccn.loc.gov/2022013430

Illustrations: Denis Alonso
Design: Diane Mielke

Printed in India

23 24 25 26 27 28/REP/10 9 8 7 6 5 4 3 2 1

A Note to Parents

What is prayer? Why do we pray? Does God really listen?

The Beginner's Bible Let's Learn to Pray is designed to help young children understand the foundations of prayer. To make this huge subject more approachable, we have divided all the information into small, easy-to-follow sections:

An introduction to prayer, pgs. 4-9

Where, when, and how to pray, pgs. 10-15

The different types of prayer, pgs. 16-48

Using *The Beginner's Bible* as a guide, we'll explore prayers of praise, request, forgiveness, complaint, and thanks. Each type of prayer includes:

- An example from *The Beginner's Bible*
- Guided questions for discussion
- Prayer prompts to help readers connect with God

Finally, there is a reference and review page so that children can easily find and recall what they've learned about prayer and then think about it a little bit more. We hope this book provides a meaningful introduction to the importance of prayer, and that it inspires readers to develop a personal, lasting relationship with God.

Do you like to talk?

Who do you talk to?

To your mom or dad?

To your brother or sister?

To a teacher or a friend?

Sometimes talking is easy, and sometimes talking is hard.

Guess what? Talking can always be easy when you talk to God!
He is with you and listening all the time.

Maybe you already talk to God.
Talking to God is called PRAYER.

There are lots of ways to pray.

You can pray out loud. You can whisper.
You can read a prayer. You can write a prayer.
You can even sing and dance and clap and jump a prayer!

God will listen to you pray, no matter how you do it.
And God's children know he is listening to them.

All the time.

No matter what.

You are one of God's very special, very loved friends!

In the Bible, we read about many of God's friends. We hear about how and why they talk to God. And we learn about how God talks right back, showing them how much he loves and cares for them.

He will do the same for you.
No matter where or when or how you pray, he will listen and respond to you!

Where to Pray

Are you sitting in a chair? Are you on a grown-up's lap? Are you lying in bed? Are you outside in a hammock? Guess what? No matter where you are, you can pray.

Remember that prayer is talking to God. And we can talk to him anywhere. How is that possible? Well, because God is everywhere!

God is in a church. He is in a classroom. He is in your bedroom and at the dining room table. God is out on the playground. He is at your neighbor's house. And God is even with you on vacation at the beach.

Does it matter where we pray? NO. Does it have to be quiet and peaceful? NO. Do you need other people praying with you? NO. Do you need to be alone with God? NO. The important thing is to PRAY.

Jesus prayed in a garden,
　　　on a boat,
　　　　　at the beach,
　　　　　　　at supper with his friends,
　　　　　　　　　and with large and small groups of followers.

ANYWHERE we pray is the right place to pray!

When to Pray

Is it bedtime? Quiet time? Are you in Sunday school or being lazy in the backyard? Are you reading with someone? Or are you all alone?

Did something big and important and happy just happen that you want to thank God for? Or are you sad and alone and trying not to cry because you are upset?

ALL of these are great times to pray. But guess what? ANYTIME is time to pray.

Good times … bad times …
    sad and happy times …
        church time, Sunday school, grace before
        dinnertime …
            even riding on the bus to school.

Every minute of every day is a time to pray to God, to say, "I love you, God," to say, "Thank you, God," or to say, "Please, God! I need your help."

How to Pray

Have you ever knelt down next to your bed to say a prayer? Did you fold your hands? Did you close your eyes? Or did you keep your eyes wide open to look out the window?

Have you ever raised up both your arms like you want to give God a big hug and prayed? Have you sat on a pillow in your quiet room and whispered to God?

Do you like to sing loudly at church during worship?
　　And clap your hands and stomp your feet
　　　　while singing a praise song to God?
　　　　　　There is no right or wrong way to pray!

God listens to you talking to him even if you write him a note, read a prayer someone else wrote, play your favorite song for him on the piano, or just close your eyes and don't say a thing. God listens if you are alone or if you are with two or three or one hundred people.

He knows you have something to say to him. He will listen to you no matter how you pray.

And even more importantly than where or when or how you pray is the fact that you can talk to God about anything and everything. It's true!

PRAISE GOD IN PRAYER

One kind of prayer is a praise prayer. Do you know what the word PRAISE means? Praise means to show someone respect, to let them know how much you like what they do and who they are.

It is a good thing to praise God! It is good to let him know how important he is in your life. According to the Bible, there are many ways to praise God. You can praise God

in a loud voice … in a soft whisper …
with singing and dancing …
banging drums and clanging cymbals …
all alone or with some friends.

God is always good.
Show him your love by praising
him any way you can!

The Israelites Praise God

Exodus 14

The Israelites were God's special people. For many years, they were slaves in Egypt. God promised he would set them free from slavery.

He got his friend Moses to help him, and after a while Pharaoh let the Israelites leave Egypt!

Soon God's people came to the shore of the Red Sea. They looked back.

"Oh, no! Here come Pharaoh's men!" they cried. "They want to take us back to Egypt!"

But God loved his people. He would save the Israelites.

Moses prayed and God pushed back the sea to make a path through the water. They all walked to the other side. But Pharaoh's army did not make it. They were swept away. God's people were safe and sound.

Moses and all the Israelites danced and sang praise to God. They were really free! They were not slaves anymore!

The Israelites wanted God to know just how important he was to them.

PRAYER TIME

Think about a time God helped you.

- Did you tell God how great he is?

- What did you say to him in your prayer?

- How did you pray?

- Were you loud or quiet?

Praise him again ...

> **Dear God, you are a loving and caring God! You freed the Israelites from slavery! You do so many good things for me too. I will never forget to tell you, "You are GREAT!"**

ASK GOD IN PRAYER

One kind of prayer is a REQUEST or petition … that is a big way to say you are asking God for something. God wants you to ask him for things. He loves you and always wants to help.

You can pray and ask God for anything. He will listen to everything you say.

You can ask God

 for help with a problem …

  to feel better … or for someone you love to get better soon …

   for something you want to have—like a puppy or a game or a baby brother.

But remember one big thing—God does not always say "yes" when we ask him for something. God knows what is best for you. He knows what you need, he knows what is safe, and he knows what is good for everyone else too. So God might say, "No, not right now," or "I have something different in mind."

But keep asking God. He wants you to trust him and his decisions.

Solomon Prays to God

1 Kings 3:1-15

Long ago, Solomon was a great king in Israel. He loved God very much. And God loved Solomon. One night, Solomon had a dream. God said, "Ask me for anything you want."

Solomon could have asked for gold and fancy clothes and a big palace. But Solomon prayed, "Please give me wisdom, God. I want to know what is right and what is wrong."

God gave Solomon the wisdom he prayed for. He became the wisest person around! But there is more!

God was happy that Solomon prayed and asked for wisdom instead of gold. So God gave him gold too! AND God gave Solomon fancy clothes, a palace to live in, and people from all around loved and respected him.

Solomon used his gifts from God to help God's people. God was happy about that too.

PRAYER TIME

Think about a time you asked God for something.

- Did you pray for something for yourself? Or for a friend?

- Did you pray about it many times?

- Did God give you an answer right away?

- Were you happy with the answer God gave you?

Ask him again ...

Dear God, I know you love me. I know you want what is best for me. Help me to always trust you and ask you for what I need. Help me to accept your answer whether you say "yes" or "no."

SAY SORRY IN PRAYER

Have you ever done something you shouldn't have? Afterward, did you ask someone to forgive you? To ask for FORGIVENESS is to say you are sorry and hope for grace or mercy. There are times it can feel hard and a little scary to ask for forgiveness. You are admitting that you did something wrong.

God gave us a special gift called free will, which means we can make choices. Sometimes we make good choices, and sometimes we make bad choices. God understands that we do wrong things because we are human and make the wrong choice once in a while. But no matter what we do, God will forgive us. We need to feel sorry in our hearts and pray to him, asking for his understanding and forgiveness.

You can say, "I am sorry, God,"

when you disobey your mom or dad …

or argue with a brother or sister …

when you take something that is not yours to use …

when you think thoughts or say things that are not kind …

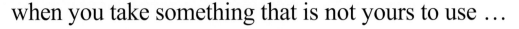

God will forgive you. He knows your heart. He loves you all the time.

Jonah

Jonah

God had a friend named Jonah. Jonah was a prophet, which means his job was to deliver God's message of love to all people. God wanted Jonah to go to a place named Nineveh, to tell those people to be good. But Jonah made the choice to say "no."

And then Jonah made another wrong choice. He ran away from God! He got on a boat. It started to storm. To stop the storm, Jonah told the sailors to throw him into the sea. They did, and the storm stopped!

God did not want his friend Jonah to be hurt, so he sent a big fish to help.

The big fish swallowed up Jonah. Jonah stayed safe in the fish for three days. And guess what Jonah did? Jonah prayed to God. "Please forgive me for making wrong choices." He was really sorry.

And do you know what happened? God forgave Jonah, of course!

The fish spit Jonah out, right on the shore. And Jonah headed to Nineveh to tell the people about God. Jonah told them, "God loves you. Stop doing bad things!"

The people did stop making wrong choices. And God forgave those people in Nineveh too!

PRAYER TIME

Think about a time you made a wrong choice.

- Did you say you were sorry?

- Was it a little hard? Was it scary?

- Did you pray to God about your choice and ask for his forgiveness too?

- Did it make you feel better?

Say sorry again ...

Dearest Lord, you know sometimes I make wrong choices. Help me to think before I speak or before I do something I shouldn't. Please know that I am trying to make good choices. I want to be good and give you glory.

COMPLAIN IN PRAYER

Sometimes things do not go the way we want them to go. Sometimes we do not get what we want. That can make us sad or mad. We might want to cry or complain or yell. What do you do when this happens? Do you tell a grown-up like your mom or dad? Do you tell a teacher or friend?

You probably hope that whomever you tell can help you fix things. Well, guess what? You should tell God about it. God wants you to pray to him. He wants you to tell him all of your problems, and he is OKAY if you want to cry and yell and be mad about the situation. You can complain to God

about the weather …

a bad hair day …

or something your brother or sister did …

or that you are sad, even
if you don't know why.

Sometimes it feels good just to say things out loud in your prayer. God knows that. He will listen no matter what.

God's People Want a King

1 Samuel 8-10

God's people wanted a king—just like other kingdoms. They wanted a king they could see. They complained about it to God's friend, Samuel.

Samuel prayed to God. "What should I do, God? Your people want a king."

God listened carefully to his people. God listened to Samuel too. God knew his people were moaning and groaning and complaining to Samuel. God knew it would not be perfect, but he still listened carefully. And then he gave the people what they moaned and groaned about—he gave them a king named Saul.

The people were happy! They finally had what they wanted. A leader they could see and follow. They felt better. They stopped complaining for a while.

Saul was a good king for a long time. But something happened. Saul made some bad choices. He was not a good king anymore. The people knew it. God knew it. Samuel prayed to God again. Eventually God gave his people another king—David.

Praying to God is important. His love is so great that he will listen to every word you say—every word you think. Even when we complain, when we are mad or sad or cry about something, he hears us loud and clear. Just like he heard his people. And he will answer. Be sure you are listening to him too!

PRAYER TIME

Think about a time you complained to someone—your mom or dad or a friend.

- Did it help to say it out loud?

- Did you tell God about your problem too?

- How do you know God hears what you have to say to him?

Go ahead and complain again ...

> **Lord, you know me. You know that sometimes I just want to complain. Help me to remember that I can always come to you. Help me remember that you want me to be happy and you will always listen—no matter what.**

GIVE THANKS IN PRAYER

Everything we have is from God. Have you ever thought about that? It's true. It is also true that we have to remember to pray and say THANK YOU to God. People in the Old Testament and the New Testament prayed to God, thanking him for so many things. They said thank you for food and water, for freedom, for victory in battles, for health and for creation and for God's love.

We like hearing people say thanks, and so does God. He loves us completely and gives us what we need. When we thank him, we let God know how much we love him right back. You can give thanks to God

out loud or in your heart ...

by singing, like in the Psalms ...

by dancing, like the Israelites ...

by respecting whatever it is God has given you.

Just never forget to say, "Thank you, God!"

The Ten Lepers

Luke 17:11-19

While Jesus was on earth, he showed people how much he loved them. He taught about God's great love. And he did special things called miracles. Miracles are actions that can only be done by God. He does miracles to show his great love for people.

While he was walking down the road one day, Jesus met ten men. The men all had sores on their skin. It was a sickness called leprosy. Most people did not like to be around others who had leprosy. But Jesus did not mind. The men all said, "Jesus, please help us! Make us better."

Jesus wanted to help them. So he cured them—the leprosy was gone! It was a miracle.

All the men were better! They ran away to tell all the people they knew the very good news.

But one man went back to Jesus. He wanted to say thank you. He wanted Jesus to know how happy he was.

And he wanted God to know how much he appreciated this great gift of feeling better!

PRAYER TIME

Think about a great gift God has given to you.
(Remember that everything is from him!)

*   How did you show God how much you appreciated his gift?

*   Did you pray to him, saying thank you?

*   Are you taking care of the gift (keeping yourself healthy, respecting nature, etc.)?

Give thanks again ...

Dear Lord, I know everything I have is from you. Thank you for this great gift. I know you love me. Please know that I love you too. I promise to respect this gift. I will use it the best way I know how. And I will share my gifts from you.

The Lord's Prayer

One day, Jesus was on a mountain teaching many of his followers. They asked him, "How should we pray?" and he answered by saying this prayer. It is called THE LORD'S PRAYER.

THE LORD'S PRAYER

Our Father in heaven,

hallowed be your name,

your kingdom come,

your will be done,

on earth as it is in heaven.

Give us today our daily bread.

And forgive us our debts,

as we also have forgiven our debtors.

And lead us not into temptation,

but deliver us from the evil one.

AMEN

When Jesus taught this prayer to his followers, he had some important messages for us. He wants us to PRAISE our Father in heaven and honor his name. He wants us to remember that we can REQUEST anything—something big, like his kingdom on earth, or something small, like our daily meals. And he wants us to pray for FORGIVENESS when we make wrong choices, and forgive those who hurt us.

Did you notice? Jesus prayed the same kinds of prayers we pray! And we can pray his special prayer, or any prayer that's in our hearts. Anywhere. Anytime. No matter what. Because God loves us, and he is listening.

Let's Review the 5 Basic Types of Prayer

Praise: Showing God respect and love through words and actions

- Look in your Bible. Find a Bible story that shows someone praising God.
- Why might you praise God?
- Say a prayer of praise to God.

Request/Petition: Asking God for something, remembering he loves you and always knows what is best

- Look in your Bible. Find a Bible story that shows someone asking God for something.
- What might you ask God to do for you?
- Say a prayer asking God for something you feel you need.

Forgiveness: Saying you are sorry to God and receiving his grace and mercy

- Look in your Bible. Find a Bible story that shows someone asking God for forgiveness
- When might you ask God to forgive you?
- Say a prayer asking God for forgiveness and grace.

Complaint: Telling God your problems and concerns, knowing he will listen and still love yc

- Look in your Bible. Find a Bible story that shows someone complaining to God.
- Why might you complain to God?
- Say a prayer telling God about a problem you need help with.

Thanksgiving: Showing God you are thankful for all of his gifts through words and actions

- Look in your Bible. Find a Bible story that shows someone thanking God.
- Why might you thank God?
- Say a prayer giving thanks to God for everything.